NATURE'S LIFE Cycles

The Life Cycle
of a
SEA TURTLE

By Anna Kingston

Gareth Stevens
Publishing

Please visit our Web site, www.garethstevens.com. For a free color catalog of all our high-quality books, call toll free 1-800-542-2595 or fax 1-877-542-2596.

Library of Congress Cataloging-in-Publication Data

Kingston, Anna.
 The life cycle of a sea turtle / Anna Kingston.
     p. cm. — (Nature's life cycles)
 Includes index.
 ISBN 978-1-4339-4688-2 (pbk.)
 ISBN 978-1-4339-4687-5 (library binding)
 ISBN 978-1-4339-4689-9 (6-pack)
 1. Sea turtles—Life cycles—Juvenile literature. I. Title.
 QL666.C536K56 2011
 597.92'8156—dc22

                                    2010031282

First Edition

Published in 2011 by
Gareth Stevens Publishing
111 East 14th Street, Suite 349
New York, NY 10003

Copyright © 2011 Gareth Stevens Publishing

Designer: Daniel Hosek
Editor: Therese Shea

Photo credits: Cover, p. 1 David Fleetham/Visuals Unlimited/Getty Images; pp. 5, 9, 11, 17, 21 (egg, adult) Shutterstock.com; pp. 6–7, iStockphoto.com; p. 21 (hatchling) Jason Edwards/National Geographic/Getty Images; p. 13 Caroline Warren/Photodisc/Getty Images; p. 15 David Silverman/Getty Images; p. 19 U.S. Navy/Getty Images; p. 21 (juvenile) Douglas D. Seifert/Taxi/Getty Images.

Printed in the United States of America

CPSIA compliance information: Batch #CW11GS: For further information contact Gareth Stevens, New York, New York at 1-800-542-2595.

Contents

Words in the glossary appear in **bold** type the first time they are used in the text.

Suited for the Sea

Sea turtles are **reptiles**. Reptiles have **lungs** and breathe air. Sea turtles' special lungs store lots of air so they can stay underwater for a long time.

Sea turtles have a shell just like land turtles have. This shell helps keep their body safe from enemies.

Sea turtles drink seawater. They have special body parts called salt glands. These glands remove salt from seawater. The turtles' bodies get rid of the salt as tears.

Sea turtles stay underwater
for up to 45 minutes!
▼

AWESOME ANIMAL!

When sea turtles are
underwater, they can see
and hear very well.

Kinds of Sea Turtles

Sea turtles live in warm ocean waters all around the world. There are several kinds of sea turtles. The most common is the olive ridley turtle. It lives in the Atlantic Ocean, Pacific Ocean, and Indian Ocean.

Different kinds of turtles eat different foods. Green sea turtles feed on sea grasses. Flatback turtles eat jellyfish and other soft-bodied sea creatures. Loggerhead turtles have very strong **jaws**. They eat hard-shelled sea creatures such as crabs and clams.

AWESOME ANIMAL!

Leatherback turtles are covered with thin, leathery skin instead of a hard shell.

Leatherback turtles are the largest sea turtles. They can be up to 6.5 feet (2 m) long!

7

Long-Distance Swimmers

Sea turtles are at home in the ocean. They are strong swimmers. They push themselves through the water with their long **flippers**. Sea turtles spend most of their lives in the water. However, all sea turtles begin their lives on land. They **hatch** from eggs laid on beaches.

Mother sea turtles travel thousands of miles to reach the beaches where they lay their eggs. Sea turtles often lay their eggs on the same beaches where they were born.

Scientists think that sea turtles may use the smell of the ocean water to figure out where they are.

Eggs

Mother sea turtles use their back flippers to dig a hole on the beach. Each mother may lay as many as 100 eggs in a hole! When the mother is finished laying the eggs, she covers them with sand. Then she crawls back into the ocean and swims away.

Sea turtle eggs are soft, round, and white. The eggshells are so thin that the **embryos** inside breathe through them. The **temperature** of the eggs decides if the turtles will be males or females.

Sea turtle eggs are kept warm in the sand.

AWESOME ANIMAL!

Warmer eggs produce females, while colder eggs produce males.

Hatchlings

About 2 months after a mother sea turtle lays her eggs, baby turtles hatch out of them. The babies are known as hatchlings. All the hatchlings in a nest break out of their eggs around the same time. Then they start climbing out of the sand. The hatchlings may have to dig through as much as 3 feet (90 cm) of sand!

As soon as the hatchlings have crawled out of the sand, they start crawling with their flippers toward the ocean.

Hatchlings almost always make their trip to the sea at night.
▼

AWESOME ANIMAL!

The hatchlings naturally head toward the sky above the ocean. It's lighter than the sky above land.

Juveniles

After the hatchlings reach the water, they swim out to sea. For the next few years, they float around the open ocean. Newly hatched sea turtles have leftover **yolk** from their eggs inside their bodies. For the first few weeks, the turtles use the yolk as food. Later, they eat tiny sea creatures.

After a few years, the hatchlings grow into **juveniles**. They spend most of their time in water near the coast. They start eating the same kinds of food as adult sea turtles.

This baby loggerhead sea turtle is about to enter the ocean for the first time. ▼

AWESOME ANIMAL!

For many years, scientists had no idea what happened to hatchlings after they entered the ocean. They called these years of a sea turtle's life the "lost years."

15

Adults

Depending on the kind of sea turtle and the place they live, sea turtles become full-grown adults between the ages of 5 and 35.

When **mating** season comes, adult sea turtles head to waters where males and females mate. Sea turtle mating grounds are usually near or on the way to beaches where females lay their eggs. After mating, female sea turtles go to their beaches and lay their eggs. The sea turtle life cycle begins again.

Male sea turtles usually reach the mating grounds first and wait for the females to show up.

17

Always in Danger

Crabs, raccoons, coyotes, and other animals dig up sea turtle eggs and eat them. Animals such as birds, crabs, and dogs catch hatchlings on the beach. Once the hatchlings are in the water, large fish and seabirds may eat them.

In the past, so many sea turtles were killed that some countries outlawed hunting them. Even today, sea turtles get caught in fishing nets and die because they can't come up to breathe.

These men are helping free some sea turtles tangled in nets.

AWESOME ANIMAL!

While many animals eat sea turtle eggs and hatchlings, adult sea turtles' shells usually keep them safe. Their main enemies are people!

19

Ways to Help

People have hurt sea turtles. When they build houses on beaches where sea turtles nest, mother turtles are scared away. Lights from buildings get hatchlings mixed up. They may head toward the buildings instead of the ocean. Some sea turtles think plastic bags in the water are jellyfish. If they eat the bags, they can die.

However, people are finding ways to help sea turtles. For example, some towns turn off lights at night during hatching season. No one wants to live without these wonderful sea creatures!

The Life Cycle of a Sea Turtle

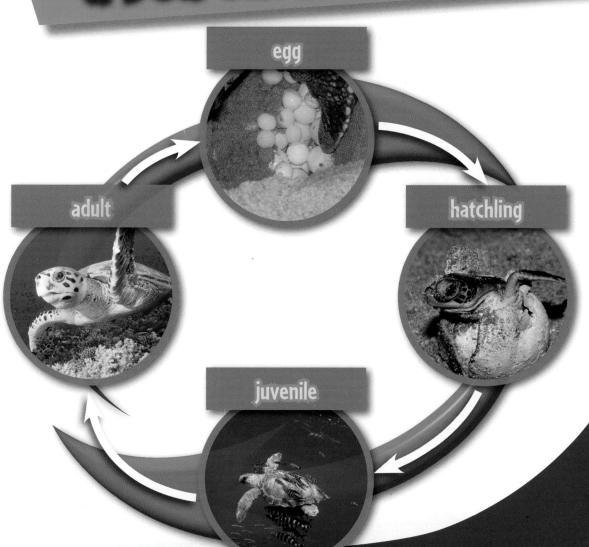

egg

hatchling

juvenile

adult

Glossary

embryo: a form of an animal before it is born

flipper: a wide, flat body part that helps an animal swim

hatch: to come out of an egg

jaw: the upper or lower part of the mouth

juvenile: an animal that is older than a baby and younger than an adult

lung: a body part that takes in air and lets it out

mating: the act of coming together to make babies

reptile: an animal covered with scales or plates that breathes air, has a backbone, and lays eggs

temperature: how hot or cold something is

yolk: the liquid inside an egg that feeds a growing baby animal

For More Information

Books

Herriges, Ann. *Sea Turtles*. Minneapolis, MN: Bellwether Media, 2007.

Rhodes, Mary Jo. *Sea Turtles*. New York, NY: Children's Press, 2005.

Swinburne, Stephen R. *Turtle Tide: The Ways of Sea Turtles*. Honesdale, PA: Boyds Mills Press, 2005.

Web Sites

Leatherback Sea Turtles

kids.nationalgeographic.com/kids/animals/creaturefeature/ leatherback-sea-turtle/

Read turtle facts, see photos, and watch videos of leatherback sea turtles in action.

Sea Turtles

www.nmfs.noaa.gov/pr/education/turtles.htm

This site has many facts on six kinds of sea turtles.

Index